wild and beautiful
Crater Lake
NATIONAL PARK

Photography by Charles A. Blakeslee *and others*

FARCOUNTRY
PRESS

Right: Llao Rock from Steel Bay.

Facing page, top to bottom:
Wildflowers at Sun Creek.
Window detail from the Crater Lake Lodge.
Frosty morning on the South Rim.

Title page: Wizard Island.

Front cover: Wizard Island from Discovery Point.

Back cover: The Phantom Ship from Sun Notch.

ISBN 10: 1-56037-182-X
ISBN 13: 978-1-56037-182-3

For more information about our books, write Farcountry Press, P.O. Box 5630,
Helena, MT 59604; call (800) 821-3874; or visit www.farcountrypress.com.

Created, produced, and designed in the United States.
Printed in Korea.

16 15 14 13 12   3 4 5 6 7

Foreword

Crater Lake National Park is the jewel of southern Oregon's Cascade Mountains. It is a beautiful and wondrous place and like nowhere else on earth.

Crater Lake became a national park on May 22, 1902, through the efforts of William Gladstone Steel, who wanted it to be protected for future generations. The 183,224-acre park is part of the greater wilderness ecosystem that encompasses Mount Thielsen Wilderness to the north and Sky Lakes Wilderness to the south.

I began my quest to explore and photograph Crater Lake National Park more than fifteen years ago, and the more I returned to this magical place, the more I discovered. Many of the places are miles away from the rim or the lake itself. I traveled from Boundary Springs in the far northwest corner of the park to Annie Creek in the south.

Crater Lake is located on the crest of the southern Cascades, with its rim at about 7,000 feet in elevation. The winter storms off the Pacific drop a prodigious amount of snow, as much as fifty feet in the long winter season. As a result, much of my photographic exploring was done on snowshoes. The rapidly changing weather patterns, so frequent at Crater Lake, make photography a challenge. But the changing light and cloud formations make it well worth the effort.

The short summer season begins in June with melting snowbanks and early wildflowers. In the later summer months, wildflowers carpet the meadows, and many species bloom in the Castle Crest area near park headquarters. In the autumn of 2000, I photographed around the crater rim and high peaks until late October, when the season's first heavy snow closed all roads but the one to Rim Village. I shall never forget a morning in early September, when from the summit of 8,054-foot Garfield Peak, I watched the sunrise across the Cascades, and the play of light from Mount Shasta in northern California to the Three Sisters in central Oregon—a distance of nearly 200 miles. Later, under an azure sky, the lake surface was like glass, and as blue as I had ever seen it.

To fellow photographers, Fred Pflughoft and David Morris: your work always shows a love and appreciation for nature and the environment. I enjoy our friendship and photographing with you both. To John Hinderman: your excellent wildlife images have made a special contribution to this book. I express my deepest thanks to all three of you.

I also thank my wife, Mary, for her support and tireless energy in captioning all my photographic images, and keeping track of where I travel.

I hope readers enjoy this photographic journey to wild and beautiful Crater Lake as much as I have enjoyed bringing it to you. — *Charles A. Blakeslee*

Looking north from Rim Village, over Crater Lake and past Wizard Island to (left to right) The Watchman, Hillman Peak, and Llao Rock.

Cloud reflection on Crater Lake's 6,176-foot-elevation surface.

Facing page: Llao Rock, named for the Klamath Indians' Lord of the Below World, and Mount Thielsen.

The well-named lava feature, The Phantom Ship, seen (facing page) from Sun Notch and (this page) from Crater Lake's surface.

Left: Viewing the birth of a new day from Discovery Point.

Below: September campers need to be prepared for cool evenings.

Right: Annie Falls traces its delicate path among trees in October dress.

Below: Aspen blazes before a grove of ponderosa pine on a sunny fall day.

Godfrey Glen on Annie Creek.

Near The Watchman, visitors can gaze past Mount McLoughlin in Oregon to Mount Shasta in California.

Facing page: The fire lookout atop The Watchman guarantees privacy for those concentrating on noticing smoke plumes.

Left: The rising moon seems to burn its way through afternoon fog on Crater Lake.

17

Above: Hillman Peak on the west side rises to 8,151 feet, highest point on the rim.

Left: Grayback Ridge Motor Nature Trail takes automobile riders closer to the sights.

Facing page: Rim Drive wanders for thirty-three miles, encircling Crater Lake and serving traffic from July to mid-October.

Crater Lake Lodge dates from 1915, but was refurbished in the mid-1990s.

Facing page: An invitation to enjoy the lodge's back porch. FRED PFLUGHOFT PHOTO

Hikers near Sun Notch on the east side of Applegate Peak.

Facing page: The brilliant pink of fireweed at Vidae Falls.

Crater Lake National Park is open to people all winter, as snowshoe tracks near the lodge attest.

Facing page: From the south rim to Mount Scott, the park's highest peak at 8,929 feet elevation.

Above: Quick to hide, pine martens are one of the park's mammals that few visitors get to see. JOHN L. HINDERMAN PHOTO

Left: November sparkles on firs of the south rim.

Facing page: Wizard Island, seen here after an autumn snowfall, was thought by Klamath Indians to be the head of Lord of the Below World, whose dismembered body was thrown into the lake by another spirit. Monsters in the water ate all pieces except the head.

Past a slope of Garfield Peak to Mount Scott.

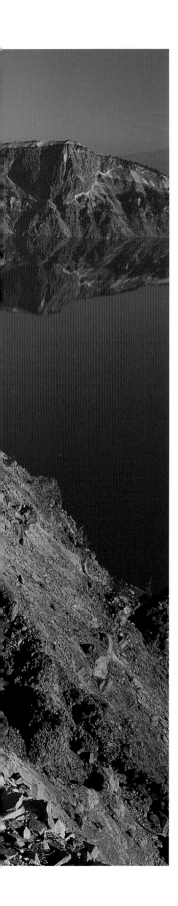

A geology lesson from Ranger Mom. FRED PFLUGHOFT PHOTO

Left: From the top of Garfield Peak, looking down into the caldera, or center of a collapsed volcano, that holds Crater Lake, the United States' deepest lake.

Facing page: Skell Channel (named for the Lord of the Above World) from The Watchman. DAVID M. MORRIS PHOTO

Below: Here, near Applegate Peak, Crater Lake's bottom is only thirty feet away; elsewhere it drops as far as 1,943 feet.

Below: Bull elk are the park's largest mammals. FRED PFLUGHOFT PHOTO

Right: South of the park's Cascade Mountains location is the Klamath Basin, as seen here from near Dutton Ridge.

From Cleetwood Cove, visitors can take boat tours or trail hikes.

Facing page: Cleetwood Cove, from the Cleetwood Cove Trail.

Above: The park's interpretive signs tell how the amazing features were formed—and may also provide a fine place for a golden-mantled ground squirrel to take a little sun.

Left: Rhyodacite, an igneous rock, of the Cleetwood Flow.

Facing page: Pumice Castle on the east rim is made of ash from the Mount Mazama explosion of 70,000 years ago that formed Crater Lake's caldera.

Left: A whitebark pine snag, twisted by the wind, from Merriam Point.

Left: Many visitors enjoy the self-guided historic walking tour, as here near Munson Creek.

Facing page: Steel Bay is named for William Gladstone Steel, who first saw Crater Lake in 1885, campaigned for its protection until the park's creation in 1902, and continued working to support the park for three more decades.

Left: Sly and shy, red foxes usually are gone at the sound of approaching humans. FRED PFLUGHOFT PHOTO

Above: Driving from park headquarters to Rim Village means experiencing The Corkscrew, viewed here from Garfield Peak.

Left: Welcome to the park's 183,224 acres for those coming from the direction of Klamath Falls, Oregon.

Facing page: Union Peak as seen from Garfield Peak early of a morning.

NATIONAL PARK SERVICE
CRATER
LAKE
NATIONAL
PARK
SOUTH ENTRANCE
U.S. DEPARTMENT
OF INTERIOR

Devils Backbone on the rim as seen from a tour boat.

Left: Wizard Island is a cinder cone formed by volcanic Mount Mazama's continued activity after the caldera was created; Mount Scott on the horizon also results from volcanic activity on the slopes of Mazama.

Left: Wildflower season in Crater Lake National Park is late and brief; this view is along Castle Crest Wildflower Trail.

Below: Delicate luncheon of wild roses for a porcupine. JOHN L. HINDERMAN PHOTO

Above and left: The Pinnacles, rising as much as 200 feet from Wheeler Creek Canyon, are eroded from volcanic rocks pumice and scoria.

Below: Bicycling is allowed on the park's paved roads. FRED PFLUGHOFT PHOTO

Right: Rim Drive heading toward views of Klamath Basin.

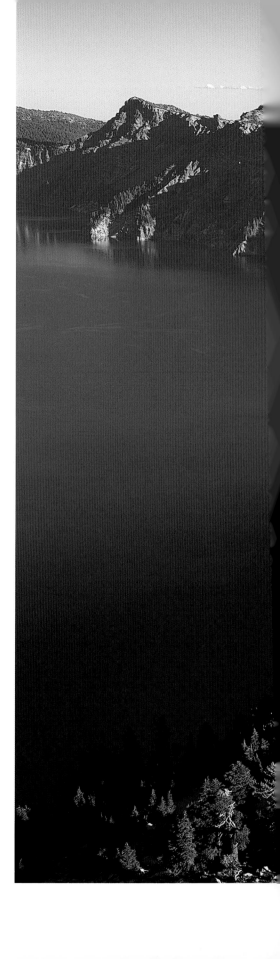

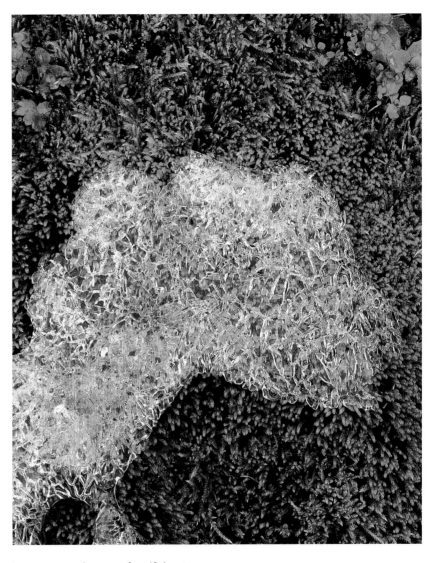

Ice on moss shapes a fanciful pattern.

Left: Wheeler Creek falls from Dutton Ridge.

Sinnott Memorial Overlook blends beautifully into its position on the rim. <small>FRED PFLUGHOFT PHOTO</small>

Above: The path to Sinnott Memorial Overlook, which includes exhibits on Crater Lake history and geology.

Left: Honoring Stephen T. Mather, first director of the National Park Service.

Left: Bobcats, recognized by their tufted ears, weigh only fifteen to twenty-five pounds, and hunt rabbits, hares, and porcupines. JOHN L. HINDERMAN PHOTO

Facing page: Flowing from Boundary Springs on the park's northwest border are the headwaters of the Rogue River.

ENTERING CRATER LAKE NATIONAL PARK
PERMIT REQUIRED
FOR BACKCOUNTRY CAMPING.
PETS, FIREARMS, VEHICLES
NOT PERMITTED.

Left: On the Boundary Springs Trail.

Right: Raccoons seem to wash their food carefully before eating.

Facing page: Ponderosa pine, aspen and fir trees near the south entrance paint an autumn scene.

Clark's nutcracker was first described for science by the Lewis and Clark Expedition. A later ornithologist named the species for Captain William Clark.
FRED PFLUGHOFT PHOTO

Left: The view of Pumice Point from Steel Bay.

Above and facing page: Lewis's monkeyflower, here along Castle Crest Wildflower Trail, was first scientifically described by Meriwether Lewis before the Lewis and Clark Expedition reached future Oregon late in 1805.

Right: Red elderberry,
in September, above
the Phantom ship.

Black bears in the park are definitely not teddy bears and must be left alone. JOHN L. HINDERMAN PHOTO

Left: Cottonwoods flourish along Annie Creek.

CRATER LAKE
LODGE

Above: Crater Lake Lodge offers a cheery welcome to the weary traveler.

Facing page: The Great Hall in Crater Lake Lodge is an example of the vernacular style of U.S. national park architecture that's come to be called "parkitecture." FRED PFLUGHOFT/DAVID M. MORRIS PHOTO

Left: A peaceful summer afternoon panorama from Scott Bluffs.

Below: If you were a blue grouse hen, this would be the world's most handsome creature, as he performs his mating display. FRED PFLUGHOFT PHOTO

Right: Tiny pikas chirp warnings to passing humans while they spend all summer spreading grass to dry and literally making hay for their winter meals.
JOHN L. HINDERMAN PHOTO

Below: Fumarole Bay from the surface of Crater Lake.

Facing page: Llao Rock rises 1873 feet above the lake's water.

Right: Red Cone is painted redder by the rising sun.

Below: A mule deer buck during the autumn rut.
JOHN L. HINDERMAN PHOTO

Seed-bearing cone of the ponderosa pine. FRED PFLUGHOFT PHOTO

Facing page: Sun Creek flows through nature's garden.

Above: Lady of the Woods, carved by Earl Russell Bush in 1917, emerges from native rock.

Right top and bottom: Crater Lake Lodge.

Mystical view from Cloudcap on an August morning.

West from Grotto Cove.

Facing page: Dutton Cliff and Garfield Peak above the Phantom Ship.

Right: This whitebark pine snag's view is, left to right, Wizard Island, Mount Shasta, Mount McLoughlin, and Hillman Peak.

Below: An approaching storm riles Crater Lake. FRED PFLUGHOFT PHOTO

The great horned owl's wingspan can approach five feet. JOHN L. HINDERMAN PHOTO

Facing page: Hemlocks standing in the fog define the Pacific Northwest ecosystem.

Moonsteps tiptoeing across Crater Lake.

Facing page: Wheeler Creek Falls in the spring.

Right: Plaikni Falls Trail, completed in 2011, guides hikers about one mile through old-growth fir and hemlock forest and past a series of rugged bluffs to spring-fed Sand Creek, which tumbles over Plaikni Falls. Plaikni is a Klamath Indian word meaning "from the high country." WILLIAM L. SULLIVAN PHOTO

Facing page: Rock formations to be found by hikers of the Garfield Peak Trail. FRED PFLUGHOFT PHOTO

Below: Pumice below Mount Scott makes for spotty flower growth.

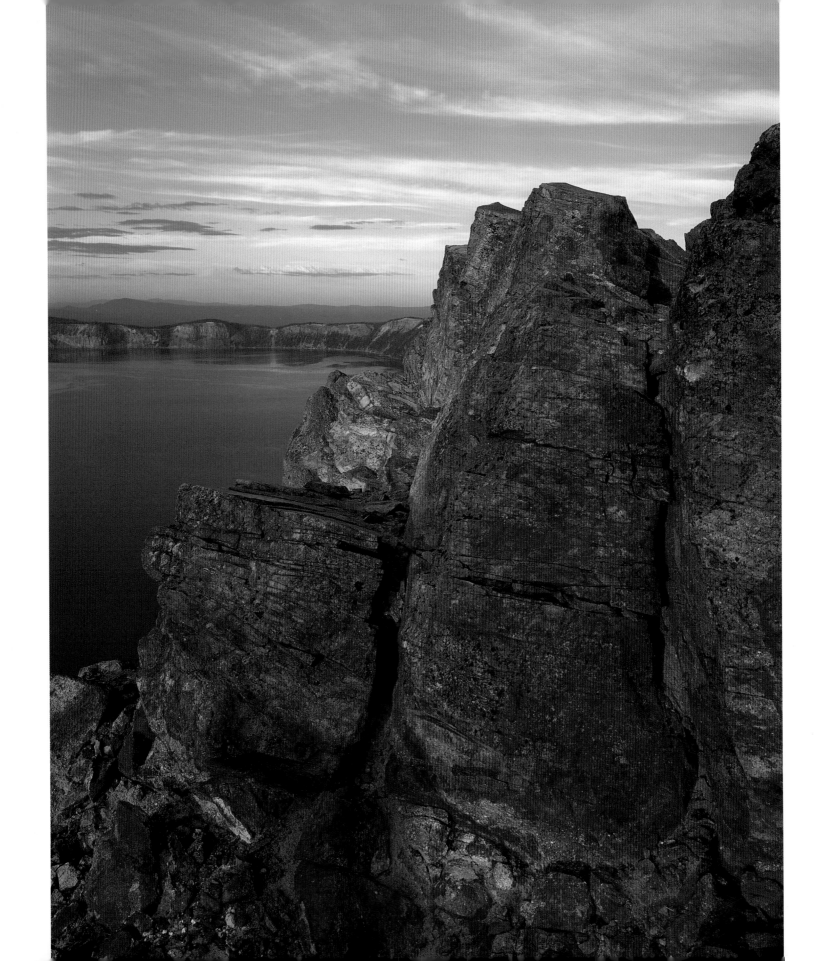

Above: Mount Scott towers in the right distance.

Winter is serious at these high elevations, with a yearly average snowfall of forty-four feet.

Facing page: Godfrey Glen after a November dusting of snow.

Stormy but enchanting November scenes of the west rim (facing page) and the south rim (above).

Left: Late-summer lightning touches down over the park's east boundary.

Below: Clouds literally flowing over Llao Rock.

Above: Looking up from Cloudcap to the advance guard of a July thunderstorm.

Left: Golden-mantled ground squirrels always seem to be very busy and very hurried. FRED PFLUGHOFT PHOTO

Facing page: Merriam Point soil frames Crater Lake. DAVID M. MORRIS PHOTO

Gray jays are also called "camp robbers," because they love to see what treats people have overlooked. FRED PFLUGHOFT PHOTO

Left: Those who attain the top of 8,054-foot Garfield Peak have this view of Crater Lake Lodge and Rim Village, 960 feet below.

A September sunset is day's end and high season's end at The Watchman fire lookout.

Preceding pages: The purple palette of dawn over Mount Scott. FRED PFLUGHOFT PHOTO